CHRIST AND THE CHRISTIAN

CHRIST AND THE CHRISTIAN

Words spoken at Keswick

BY

H. C. G. MOULE, D.D.

Bishop of Durham

"That life which I now live in the flesh, I live in faith, the faith which is in the Son of God, who loved me and gave Himself up for me,"—*Gal. ii. 20, R.V.*

WIPF & STOCK · Eugene, Oregon

To

THE DEAR AND HONOURED MEMORY OF

EVAN HENRY HOPKINS,

MY FRIEND AND HELPER IN THE LORD

Wipf and Stock Publishers
199 W 8th Ave, Suite 3
Eugene, OR 97401

Christ and the Christian
Words Spoken at Keswick
By Moule, Handley C.G.
ISBN 13: 978-1-4982-9249-8
Publication date 3/8/2016
Previously published by Marshall Brothers, 1919

PREFACE.

THIS little volume contains sermons and addresses delivered by me during the Keswick Week of 1919. They appear in the order of actual delivery. The first sermon was preached in St. John's Church, Keswick, on Sunday morning, July 20th; the second in Crosthwaite Church on the evening of the same day. Of the addresses the first was given in the Tent, on Monday evening; the second also in the Tent, on Tuesday at noon; the third in the Pavilion, on Tuesday evening; the fourth in the Tent, at the early Prayer-Meeting on Wednesday.

I have revised the printed reports to ensure final correctness. Here and there a short passage has been omitted, where the reference was only to some detail of the moment. Otherwise the matter has been left unaltered, even where, in one or two instances, a repetition of incident or illustration occurs. It seemed best to present each utterance to the reader just as it was spoken.

For me the memory of this year's Keswick Week is a precious spiritual possession. Duty called me away on the Wednesday, and I know the latter days of the Convention by report only. But I rejoice to be well assured that those days were at least as rich in life and power as the earlier time. All that I personally heard and saw was full of help and cheer.

Not least welcome was the presence of a great number of young men and women, evidently for the most part "first attenders." Experienced members of the Convention said that for many years they had not seen anything like this large representation of the new age. A brighter omen for the future there could not well be.

"One generation shall praise Thy works to another, and shall declare Thy mighty acts."

HANDLEY DUNELM.

Auckland Castle, November, 1919.

CONTENTS.

"The prophets, do they live for ever?"

"I am He that liveth for evermore."

I.

Keswick's Message in the New Age.

"If a man purge himself from these, he shall be a vessel unto honour, sanctified, and meet for the Master's use."—2 *Tim.* ii. 21.

WE meet before God to-day on an occasion sacred of course to us all, as we are Christian worshippers, but also, for many of us, filled with a special spiritual anticipation, aroused by a long tradition of blessing shed on the assemblies of Keswick. To some the hour is nothing less than thrilling with the holy memories of this place and time.

It is forty-four years since Harford Battersby, a name always dear and beautiful to his favoured friends, called together the first small Convention. With one solitary exception since that far-off 1875, the exception of 1917, Keswick has seen repeated annually a like "gathering together unto the Lord." A few, a very few here present, I presume, can recall the whole long series. Many more, like myself, can cast thought back over the larger part of the period. To all such, and to the many others whose recollections are briefer but not less deep, the very name of this town is hallowed. At Keswick—in tent, and hall, and chamber, and on the hills and beside the waters, and not least within this beautiful sanctuary of worship—they have met, they have seen, the Lord. Perhaps for the first time, perhaps by way of blissful renewal or profound development, they have entered into the awe, the joy, the power, of His secrets of holiness. Here perhaps they have been shown *themselves* with a stern disclosure, finding out in a new consciousness how the self-spirit had stained and steeped their very service of their Lord, how partial had been their obedience, how reserved their surrender, how faint at best their *Amen* to that ancient word of peace and power: "His service is perfect freedom." And then, perhaps as they have listened in the tent, perhaps as they have knelt in St. John's, or alone, it may be, in some quiet room apart, behold, the Lord has discovered Himself to the self-discovering soul. "Depart from me, for I am a sinful man." "Fear not ; I, the Son, will make thee free indeed ; I will make thee free in the act of binding thee absolutely to myself."

So the man, or the woman, has gone away from Keswick to common life. This paradise of Nature has been exchanged for " the unlovely street," the solemnly glad assembly for the secular-seeming toil and stress of modern duty, professional, industrial, pastoral, domestic—for surroundings pitilessly exacting, for atmospheres in themselves alien. But the change has served only to let the disciple find that the discovered Christ is peace and victory everywhere and for everything. Aye, the soul has come even to welcome the problem, the obstacle, the heavy load, the bitter grief, as an occasion for His power ; even as the swimmer, or say rather the wearer of the life-belt, can welcome the heave of the wave which, as he rides it, tests and proves his buoyant security.

Here all these four-and-forty years Christians innumerable have thus found themselves and have been found of their Lord. The twofold finding, exactly in proportion to its truth and depth on both its sides, has sent them back into life, for one result, meek and lowly in heart. They have not left Keswick to disgrace its name by advertising themselves as holy. They have so seen Christ as to grasp in Him the certainty that every moment they need the shelter of His atoning Cross; that in the light of the eternal holiness their very tears want washing. They can sing, and can mean the song :—

> " All, all the gifts we bring,
> And all the vows we make,
> And all the acts of love
> We plan for Thy dear sake,
> Into Thy pardoning thought,
> O God of mercy, take."

Just in proportion to their response to the real voice of Keswick they have come to love the lowest place, not only at the feet of their Redeemer, but in fellowship with their brethren. They have seen, in some gracious way, led and enlightened by the Spirit, the liberty of self-surrender, the joy and beauty of humblest service, the happiness of a convinced esteem of others as better than themselves. So the last thing likely to mark their discipleship is the accent of the critic, the attitude of the partisan of self. But then, on the other hand, on the other side of the spiritual phenomenon, these lowly souls have been found also, in the use of a strength not their own, more than conquerors over the world, the flesh, and the devil. They have proved invincibly faithful to duty, the humble duty, the difficult duty. They have been calmly courageous for unpopular righteousness and unfashionable faith. They have been, on occasion, such faithful soldiers of Christ on moral and spiritual battlefields as only those can be who can speak the witness-word, who can live the witness-life; in whose weakness dwells a trusted Christ, He whom they know as at once their generous Liberator and their absolute Possessor. His hand at the same moment keeps them from the enemy and wields them for His own adorable and beloved will.

Yes, this place has always sent out into life and service disciples of its school thus taught and qualified by Him whom our gatherings exist to glorify. Can it be other, then, than a place of memories and affections unspeakably dear to those who, like me, have long been allowed to watch its work? Some of us indeed, I know it for myself, once had our misgivings about Keswick, as if it taught a strange Gospel. We ventured, perhaps, even to pose as its critics. And here, no doubt, as in everything below the sky, all has not always maintained the ideal. Keswick has not always seen all its people so true to its true message as never to invite a legitimate anxiety. But I dare to affirm, against all exceptions, the prevalence of a noble rule. Who shall count those who have found the voice and touch of God through the saints who have ministered to us here in tent and in church? To me the very air of the place seems almost bright with the familiar but transfigured faces of dear teachers gone. I seem to see them as I recite the names—a Battersby, a Wilson, a Bowker, a Fox, an Elder Cumming, a Figgis, a Macgregor, an Evan Hopkins. They made their Master glorious to us, as they not only spoke of Him, but witnessed, in their sanctified while sincerely human being, to His reality, His fair beauty, His absolute claim, His willing grace, His everlasting affection.

But do not let me seem as if I would spend these precious moments on recollections only, even when the recollections touch those departed guides who to me, for one, spoke the word of God, and whose faith, whose creed of Holiness by Faith, I fain would follow, considering the end and exit of their course of life. I realize with all my heart the supremely practical importance of our assembly of this week, in view of the call and the needs of to-day, and of the long unknown to-morrow. And indeed, in what I have said already, my aim all along has borne full upon that thought. I have invited you to recall what Keswick has long done in the field of spiritual life, with two main purposes in view. On the one hand, I have wanted to quicken in all my friends the prayer and the purpose that the message, the ideal, of Keswick should be kept absolutely true to-day to its wonderful yesterday. And I want, on the other hand, to indicate, in the light of our retrospect, as forcibly as I can, how thus, and only thus, but thus in a grandly operative fashion, Keswick may make its solid contribution to the highest good of the to-day and the to-morrow of Church and of world, in this unexampled crisis of the story of mankind.

My first appeal, then, is for your care and prayer that the message of Keswick shall maintain an unbroken continuity, as the Convention sets out again, renewed in scale and strength, at the very date of the celebration of the Peace Treaty of the world.

That message, as we have been recollecting, is altogether distinctive. It is nothing if not profoundly spiritual. It is gathered up, as to its life and essence, into the doctrine of the revealed relations between the Christian and the Christ with a view to holiness of heart, that is to say, rightness of adjustment of the inner man towards God, issuing in holiness of life, that is to say, rightness of adjustment of temper and conduct to the whole will of the true Master of the man.

What, stated with regard to its essentials only, is the message of Keswick upon Holiness?

Let me preface the answer by quoting a summary of the Gospel, written eighty years ago by a saint indeed, Robert M'Cheyne of Dundee: "Christ for us is all our righteousness before a holy God; Christ in us is all our strength in an ungodly world."

in the New Age.

I know not how better to give in its vital essence the Keswick message than in those words. The first limb of the statement refers rather to what Keswick takes for granted than what it distinctively teaches. But it takes it for granted with such a reverential emphasis, that it is well to recall it here and now as a note inseparable from the harmony of the message.

That message then, from the first, has held fast, as for its life, to the old, the apostolic, the eternal, truth of "Christ for us, our righteousness before a holy God." It has confessed and affirmed without wavering the remission of our sins because of the blood of the Lamb; the believer's peace with God, not according to his works, whether before or after his conversion, but according to the transcendent merits of his glorious Head, who gave Himself for us, the propitiation for our sins.

There, ever and to the end, as to his peace of justification, rested Harford Battersby. For there only, and always there, the human soul which has really seen itself in the light of its holy Creator can really rest. That is the apostolic truth.

That, till Skiddaw and Derwentwater shall witness our gatherings no more, shall be the truth of Keswick, by the grace of God.

To-day, if I see things aright, to-day more than ever if possible, that resolve is called for. Partly as a result of the convulsions and sacrifices of the war, and of the mighty call of a new era for all possible mutual service in human life, but under whatever influences, it matters not—another ideal has emerged even in regions of Christian activity. It is as if not a few zealous souls were leaving behind the Gospel of the man's salvation through the great mercy of God in His crucified Son our Head, and were taking up with a Gospel according to which the man is accepted because he has been self-sacrificingly serviceable to his fellows; he may look to stand unashamed before the Throne because of his patriotic valour or his social devotion.

Now we will remember, not with harsh impatience indeed, but with a spiritual resolve, that that is not the Gospel of the Lord Jesus Christ. It handles great and sacred facts; but it altogether misplaces them. It forgets the sinfulness of sin. It ignores the awful holiness of the eternal will. It tacitly declines its *Amen* to the apostolic word, in its fathomless simplicity, "Believe on the Lord Jesus Christ and thou shalt be saved." It has little place for the utterance of the Son Himself to the Father: "This is the life eternal, to know Thee, and Jesus Christ whom Thou hast sent."

"Christ for us is all our righteousness before a holy God." So Keswick has confessed all through its story. So shall it unalterably confess and witness, even to the end.

But now we recollect that the distinctive message of our Convention, the matter of its positive testimony in the Christian Church, is that which speaks itself out in the second limb of M'Cheyne's pregnant saying: "Christ in us is all our strength in an ungodly world." So the young Scottish prophet wrote, a long generation before our Convention arose. He did not wait for Keswick to learn the apostolic verity of victorious holiness through an indwelling Saviour. And when the Convention came, what it did was not vainly to invent a novelty. It only brought out into the foreground of common faith a golden treasure of ancient

Scriptural truth and life, too often neglected or forgotten. The God-given work of Keswick, for it was indeed God-given, was only to emphasize with a new accent of decision, to put in terms of light before the common Christian's heart, this wonderful but authentic and orthodox Gospel for the inner life. The Convention teachers only said, but then they said it as if upon the housetop, that there is just one divine secret for heart-whole obedience, with all its rest and power, and that secret is the trusted Christ Himself, deep within the heart.

The saints of Keswick's early days made noble discoveries for themselves of that open secret. True men and Christians as they were, they had longed before with great desire to please God always, to run always the path of loving obedience and not be weary, to walk always in it and not faint, to be kept always from falling, alike under great temptation and in the common hour, to march continuously at liberty, keeping His commandments. And now they found, one by one, that wonderful things in that direction, humbling but unspeakably gladdening, could be done within, when, with a great simplicity of surrender, they called their Lord in to write His will on their submissive hearts, to hold His tempted servants up in His own almighty hands while He trod their tempter under His feet.

For His sake, for His glory, they ventured all their weight upon His keeping power, and they found that it bore. And they rejoiced with great and holy happiness. And they told the secret out to other men.

I have spoken of that secret as to its inmost essence only. Attendant upon it, related livingly to it, those men saw other shining truths. They saw much, and they said much, of the Holy Spirit's power and work ; His filling, with a peaceful plenitude, the inner world, lifting and controlling the whole man ; above all, revealing Christ as beloved Master of all the being. They saw, and they taught, upon another side, that this life of faith, this experience of hallowing victory through a trusted Christ, means no moral passivity, no indolence of soul. He who would live at liberty through a trusted Lord must " stir himself up to lay hold on Him." He must watch, pray, ponder the sacred Word, discipline himself in all things, if he would use his secret as only the wakeful can.

But, nevertheless, the secret itself was just this—Holiness by Faith, a life humbly true to God, made possible, made actual, by the use for victory of the trusted Christ within.

That secret, open as the love of God can make it, has been the message of Keswick from the first. It shall be so still, in the light and power of the Spirit, even to the last.

Now, moving to a close, let me lay on my brethren that other burthen of the Lord which is laid on me, so I think, by Him to-day. These altogether spiritual watchwords of our assemblies, are they after all timely for this time of ours, this epoch of earthquake, with the hopes and fears that gather over the possibilities of boundless change? Does not the new age want new wine? Does it not demand, after all, a gospel of social action rather than of spiritual mystery?

I dare to reply that never was the message of Christ and of the Spirit more vital to the progress and the health of human life. The vaster the disturbance of the world, moral and material alike, the more necessary to that world, if it is not to develop downward and to waste and wither upward, are "the powers of the world to come." The more does humanity need the breath of the Spirit of holiness, the manifestation to men's souls of the Christ of the Cross, and of the glory, and of "that blessed hope," the second coming of the Beloved, in no figurative fashion, down the opened skies. And how shall those "powers" be best injected into the troubled manhood of to-day? Through the mighty multiplication everywhere of living results, in men's and women's lives, of the reality of the better "powers"; through the presence everywhere, amidst the forgetting or rebelling multitudes, of neighbours and comrades who live a genuine human life, but live it beyond all mistake as those whose steadfast peace is Christ for us, and whose power for more than victory over sin within and sin around, for service, for sympathy, cost what sacrifice and suffering it may, is Christ within us.

Again and yet again God has saved the world from itself by a reanimated Church. And what has been His main means for the reanimation of the Church? The increase of the host of those who are indeed His own, and their glorious inspiration by the breath of His mighty grace.

Through His servants thus divinely enabled, in many a memorable instance in the past, He has wrought great social victories, great deliverances from wrong and from vice. In instances vastly more numerous, through the lives in every age of His glorious rank and file of saints, He has saved the world from itself as the salt saves from corruption the mass it penetrates.

So let us look back, look up, in this last moment, upon our text: "If a man purge himself from these, he shall be a vessel unto honour, sanctified, meet for the use of the Master," the *Despotēs*, the absolute Possessor. If he finds heart-purity, life-purity, in a trusted Christ, he shall find it not for himself alone. He shall be a vessel; he shall be fit to be carried, and to be a carrier; to bear about, in the sovereign hand of love, the commendation of God to men. He may be large, he may be very little, but he shall in any case be a "vessel *unto honour*," the golden implement of a plan and purpose infinitely honourable. His Lord shall find in him just what He wants for use. For through him, as he goes forth out of self for others, God Himself shall wonderfully go forth. Strong in a spirit-life whose living and perpetual cause is hid with Christ, he shall be employed by that Christ, whether he knows it or not, for the souls, the lives, the world, about him. Out of his joys and his griefs, out of his life and his death, shall be wrought a heavenly plan of good. And at last he shall see, in the unveiled presence of the King, that the more, in truth and depth, the life of his life was the trusted Christ, the more was his mortal course one fair and fruitful service of his generation, according to the will of God.

II.

The Living Stone and the Living Stones.

"To whom coming, as unto a living stone .... ye also, as living stones, are being built up."—1 *Pet.* ii. 4, 5.

WE have here a passage in which our Lord and Master is described under imagery which is, as I think, unique. "A living stone." This presentation of the Christ has no exact parallel, as far as I remember my Bible, anywhere else. In many places we have Him before us as the Rock, as the Stone; the Rock of Ages, the Foundation Stone, the Stone on which it is good to build, with which it is death to collide. And again and again we have the Lord before us as not merely *living*, but *the Life:* "Christ, which is our life." But in this remarkable passage we see the two views converging into one. We have the Rock, and it is alive. We have the Life, and it is embodied in the grandeur and solidity of the Rock. Then we have a like title applied to the disciples of this wonderful Christ: "living stones." To them also is attached and attributed the solidity, the stedfastness, the immovability, of rock; to them also is assigned the presence and the power of life. Once again the life is embodied in the rock, and the rock is instinct with the life. Then the text further tells us how these glorious characters of the Christ are to be injected and transfused into the man; how the Christian is, in this respect, to get to be like the Christ.

It is this presentation of what the Lord is, and what the disciple may be, and how he shall so be, that I ask to put before you as a message to-night.

There are two thoughts connected with the present moment which will make our meditation timely. First, we have now in being the great Convention, once more, in its ancient scale and strength, assembled in this well-beloved place. For Keswick and its surroundings are well-beloved indeed to Christian hearts beyond number, in this and in many a distant land. For four-and-forty years now this has been the scene annually, with one exception, of these gatherings which, beginning on a small scale under the saintly Harford Battersby, grew in due time, because they so evidently met a profound spiritual need, to the great scale they afterwards reached, and which is being renewed this year.

I take it that we have in my text a Convention message, straight from the Master. What do our meetings exist for? They exist to be a means in His hands of developing the Christlikeness of Christians; of making the man or the woman who bears the name of the self-sacrificed Son of God *like Him*, in purpose, in character, in bearing towards life and towards other people; of developing in the Christian soul a wholeness of purpose to be true to God, and then, for the Lord God's sake, to be true to men. We worship a God who is supremely the Self-Sacrificer, who looked upon the things of others, who gave Himself for them. So the Christian, in true correspondence to His life and His love, is called to live a life which is not unto self, but unto the Master first, and unto the neighbour next. For that is the ideal of Christian Holiness—a life in correspondence with the loving will of God, and spent for God upon the neighbour. There is no other life which is really true to the ideal of that great word *Christian;* the life of the being that belongs to the Christ, that has found refuge and forgiveness in the Christ, that has found life and victory over self in the Christ, that has found in the Christ the inmost and most adorable Friend of the soul which looks beyond this life to being with Christ for ever and seeing Him as He is, the King in His beauty, the essence and the heart of heaven. We shall find here, then, something true to the Keswick ideal of the Christian message, for the text tells us what the Christian is meant to be because of the Christ, and how from the Christ he may get the power so to be.

Then secondly I remember indeed the crisis of the nation and of the world at which we stand. I looked with admiring but also solemn thoughts, under the summer midnight yesterday, at the glorious illumination of the mountains. I recall ancient times of illumination after war; my memory, for example, goes back to the Crimean peace and the lighting up of things then. But never assuredly have I seen anything so beautiful and majestic in its way as this sudden splendour kindled on the hills of this paradise of nature. But I felt almost as much the solemnity as the gladness of the sight; for if this is the greatest peace that was ever made, as regards its terms and its hopes, it finds us also at a time when the anxiety of the future is at least as much upon our hearts as the gladness of it. Seldom—I do not think ever—within my long memory did England heave with such possible earthquakes of unrest as precisely at the time when we are lighting earth and sky with the lamps of peace. A time like this needs—what does it need above all things? It needs the Christian element infused into human life in as large a measure as possible. The supreme means for reconstruction, if I read things aright, will be the immense development of the spiritual temple of God, which is His true disciples banded together for His purposes and His will. The salvation of our country and of the world at this time from the result of the great War, which will be far more a disaster than a victory without Him—the salvation of our country and of the world will lie in the multiplication of the right type of Christian disciple in vast numbers ; " living stones," builded together, and lending alike their life and stability to a sorely needing world.

With these words of preface, let me come now without more ado to the text, and lay it before you, almost with the simplicity of its own inspired self, and remind you of just these facts : The Source, and the Reception, and the Power, of Spiritual Life.

First, then, we will look at this description of the Lord. He is the " living *Stone,*" Christ the rock, Christ the mighty, the immovable, the everlasting ; " Jesus Christ the same yesterday, to-day and for ever " ; the fact that can never be shaken, the supreme, the all-embracing fact. For the Lord is not merely a fact in the world of being ; the world of being exists in the fact of Him. It is said of a mediæval saint, Juliana of Norwich, that she once had a vision of her Lord. There was in His hand a small round thing, " about the size of a filbert nut," and it was told her that that was " all things that had been made " ; it was the created Universe. The relation of the created Universe to the eternal Christ was as the relation of a small thing held in the hand to the mighty man who holds it.

"Gentle Jesus, meek and mild, look upon a little child." I have heard dear children sing, this afternoon, those sweet words with their sweet voices, and they went through my soul. We shall never get beyond that child-truth—the "gentle Jesus, meek and mild." Not only the child wants Him; the old broken heart wants Him, and the old bewildered mind wants Him; and the man in the strength and fulness of life must surely know enough about himself, and about other things, to feel that he too wants divine gentleness when his soul is sore. But let us recollect that, while this is one infinitely precious side of the truth of our Master, there is this side of majesty and of might with it all, giving it all its infinite value. He is the Rock of Ages, against which the stream of immeasurable time is but a puny rivulet as it flows round Him who is the same for ever and ever. The "perpetual mountains" are but shadows and passing clouds to this Lord eternally the same. Let us thank Him for that.

But then, this wonderful Lord Christ, the Rock that cannot change or shake, "the Rock that never crumbled yet," the Rock on which it is so good to rest and so good to build, is, we see here, wonderfully more than Rock. He is the *living* Stone, the *living* Rock. The apostle does not trouble himself to reconcile the imagery; he leaves it to faith to put it right, to take the two great truths as to the Lord Christ and accept them both together; they will fit spiritually into each other at once. This Rock lives. This Rock has a heart to love, this Rock has a mind to plan for good and blessing, this Rock has arms to embrace, and a paternal tenderness, yea, and a maternal, for "as one whom *his mother comforteth*, so will I comfort you." This Rock has eyes to see deep into our inmost need, and ears to hear the least perceptible sigh of our troubled hearts. It is the living Rock, it is the loving Rock; it is a Rock whose stability is but a tool in the hands of its love, whose mass is but the implement of its mercy.

Then in the same way we come, as the next element of our text, to the Christian. He is a "living stone," a "living rock," in his measure, in his scale, in the sense in which what is absolutely true of the Lord can be true in measure of His disciple.

Here is the ideal of a Christian. First, he is a "stone," he is a "rock." He is intended to have stedfastness, immovability; a will for right that cannot be shaken; a purpose, not to be turned aside, of fidelity and absolute truthfulness of service. Here is the primary call to the disciple of the Lord the Righteous—to be absolutely for right, so that you shall always know "where he (or she) is"; so that that person's word can be absolutely trusted; so that that person's principles will bear microscopic inspection; so that the accounts of that Christian may have the noonday let in upon them, should there be need; so that the secret hours and private habits of that Christian will bear close inspection, and prove pure, self-disciplined, and true; so that that Christian as a friend is found to be the same in the day of adversity, which finds friends out, as in that of prosperity; so that that Christian shall be found willing, if the call comes, to be true to unpopular righteousness, and true to the despised faith, which is not of the world, and yet the greatest blessing to the world.

But, then, this same Christian is not to be a being of hardness and of angles. I remember a friend once saying: "They tell me that that man is a Christian, but a disagreeable one; and," he added, "that seems to me a contradiction in terms." He may have had in his mind the saying of a great and heart-winning saint whom it was once my privilege to meet, Andrew Bonar, of Glasgow. "I do not think," said Bonar, "that a man can be very holy if he is not very kind." And so the strong-principled life will not be the life which bids others, so to speak, stand off because it is so strong. Its strength, like its Lord's, will be but the implement of its loving-kindness, its unselfish serviceableness on behalf of others. There will be the same mind in it that was in Christ Jesus, who looked from the throne upon the things of others, and, because of others, made Himself of no reputation, and, because of others, became obedient, even to the length of death, and that the death of the Cross. In the strength of the true Christian (we shall presently see where and how he finds it) there will be always a sweetness and a gentleness of insight, a large view of others' weaknesses, sorrows, and needs—the noblest characteristic of the truest strength. Oh, happy the home that has such "living stones" in it. Happy the community, be it parish, or yard, or mine, that has a structure of such "living stones" building up in it. Happy the country that shall find them multiplied to a degree which makes them an appreciable element in the population. That will do more for the stability, aye, for the material prosperity, of that country, it will certainly do more for its highest form of happiness, gladness, and good, than any laws or certainly any forcible revolution could ever possibly do.

But let us remember, as we pass on now to the closing thought, that here is a picture in the Word of God not of an unattainable perfection but of what the plain Christian is meant to be. This is not the ideal for a few select souls. These are just the sound "stones" which the Master wants in great numbers for the building of His spiritual temple. They are not gems, to be let in by way of decoration; they are the common materials for the mighty structure. And the call to us who name the name of Christ is stedfastly to aim, each one of us, if we can find God's secret, at being a "living stone." Yes, we are each somehow to be a human being who, in St. Paul's words, is on the one hand "stedfast and unmovable," like a rock, and, on the other, "always abounding," that is to say, *outflowing*, "in the work of the Lord," like a river; letting self run out in living helpfulness in His Name.

But now, what is our closing theme? It is St. Peter's word, "To whom *coming*." That is the way to become a "living stone," and the way to remain a "living stone." It is to come, and come again, to the Living Stone. And the way to become fit to be builded together with other "living stones," to be amalgamable, not an isolated unit, but a being which loves co-operative sacrifice, the fellowship of life and purpose, is to be still coming to the Living Stone.

"To whom coming." There is a whole Gospel implied in that word. There is the first coming to Christ, by the soul which has discovered itself in conviction of sin, and has come to realize that the one pardon, the one peace, the one safety, the one shelter from the lightning of Eternal Holiness aggrieved, is to come to Jesus; that there is no other refuge to go to but the crucified Christ; no other answer to the accuser but "Jesus died," said by the soul which has given itself over to that Lord Jesus to be saved in His way. Then there is the continued coming of the believer, who wants spiritual strength, power, and victory, against the devil, the world, and the flesh. The one true secret for that great gift also is to come to Jesus; there alone is the divine talisman of victory. A dear and honoured friend of mine, at Keswick, long ago, as we were talking together about the work of God, and especially thinking how to help young men fiercely tempted to go wrong as to purity, described to me his experience. "God kept me in my young days" (they were the young days of a very vigorous man), "He kept me clean all through; and this is how He did it. The devil whispered often to my heart; 'Sin is sweet; other young men sin; why not you?' Then something moved me always to shut my eyes, and say to myself, in my soul, 'JESUS CHRIST.' As I pronounced the blessed Name, the temptation seemed dead under my feet, and the tempter gone." So the man came, and came again, for power and victory over evil, to the Living Rock, and he found himself a "rock," through the Rock which had touched him and given Itself to him; so, even so, he was more than conqueror.

There is nothing for which, in the course of life, such a soul will not come to Christ. It will come for light in darkness, for cheer in sadness, for safety in success, for hallowing of joy, for the turning of life's mercies not into temptations away from, but into fresh reasons for clinging to, the Lord who gives them. It must come to Him for it all. So it must be a perpetual coming.

It is not often, it may be thought, that a point of grammar sheds a spiritual light, but it does so here. The Greek word used by St. Peter for "coming" is cast into a verbal form which implies not a single, solitary, isolated arrival, as when a hunted fugitive takes refuge in a castle, once for all. The inflection of the word here implies repetition, continuity. It signifies a coming again, a coming always, a coming (shall I say?) almost with the instinctive frequency with which we draw our breath; certainly with the continuous regularity with which, on the whole, we take our food. It suggests our incessantly coming to the Rock for strength, and to the Life for life, asking Him every day to begin with us again. What I find in my own latter days, more and more, is that the one way, certainly for me, is every day to beseech the Lord to begin His processes of mercy, as to their essence, over again; again to show the soul its need, again to show it His power to save, and then again to let in the life-stream of His indwelling Self upon the springs of thought and will; to make Himself again, as if never before, the Lord both of the joys and the sorrows of the life He has given. Lay it thankfully to heart. This is what we are invited to do. It is the word of the apostle who knew so well about it himself. He came to Jesus, not only first, in obedience to the first great call; he realized that he must be coming to Him always, that he must meet his Master again, continually, and throw himself afresh at

His feet and upon His heart. This is what we are bidden to do, in a command sent straight from the heart of the Christ. For remember, there is no one so immeasurably willing to meet half-way the soul that comes to Him as the Lord Jesus Christ. He is not only a mysterious Power whom we have to approach in adoring humbleness, as indeed our spirits do when they see the majesty of the Son; He is also *the Lover* of the soul. He takes a yearning interest in us. He has a profound *affection* for us—to use a very human word. The love of Christ is not a cryptic something other than human; it is affection, pure affection, carried to its utmost height and depth. He loves to help, He loves to answer, He loves to give out His power into our weakness, and His life into our death.

> " Lord, Thou art life, though I be dead;
> Love's fire art Thou, however cold I be;
> Nor heaven have I, nor place to lay my head,
> Nor home, but Thee."

And He will delight to meet us thus "to the uttermost," to the last day of our need, to the last depth of what that need may be.

Let me close with an incident which may seal upon our hearts this faithful willingness of the Lord Jesus Christ, as it was once revealed to a very simple soul, but so revealed that I know not who may not learn afresh from it. Very long ago I was told, by a lady in my native region, this incident of her father's life. He was a saintly Nonconformist minister, in the hilly country of the west of Dorset. A gipsy clan pitched its tents in his neighbourhood, and the good man soon went among them, seeing what he could do for his Lord. He found the son of the old chief very ill, gone far in consumption. The youth could read a little; the good pastor taught him to read better, and gave him a large-print Testament; and he was permitted to lead him to the feet of Jesus. In a short time the encampment moved, going all along the south of England to Kent, and nothing passed for some while between them and their faithful friend. Then there came one day to the pastor's door a white-headed gipsy, the chief of the little camp. He asked to see the gentleman, and then produced a book. It was the

Testament given to his son. "My poor lad told me to give you this book, and to tell you to look through it. There are places marked with a burnt stick from the fire, where the words did good to his soul. I cannot read a letter. You must look and see. But there is one place, he said, where you will find *two marks.* They are against the words that did most good of all to him." And behold, the place was Heb. vii. 25: "He is able to save them to the uttermost that come unto God by Him."

"Able to save them to the uttermost"; from everything they really want saving from; to the uttermost need, and to the uttermost of their time of need.

Yes, He is able to save them that simply *come* to God by Him. Friends, brethren, sisters, may we lead the life of perpetual comers. It will never be in vain. We shall approach perpetually the Eternal Rock and find that It has arms to clasp us to its love. And the more and the oftener we come, and the closer we cling, and the more we let that power have its way, the more shall we ourselves be "living stones," good for our generation's service, and meeting the purposes of that Living Stone who let Himself be riven and stricken by the lightning of the law for us, that out of the rift for ever might flow into us His life.

III.

Possessing our Possessions.

I WILL read a few words from one of the very short Bible books, Obadiah. Here is the seventeenth verse of his one chapter: "Then shall they possess their possessions." The words imply that it is possible to have possessions unpossessed, to have what we do not know, to have what we do not use, and which is therefore as if we had it not.

One great aim of Keswick from the first has been to teach us, in the spiritual life, to possess our possessions, to realize what the Christian has credited to him as wealth, and what the call is to the Christian to use the wealth which is credited, and not to leave it asleep. Upon this I wish to speak to-night in this great gathering in the dear Keswick tent, a tent which to some of us is full beyond description of the population of memory, but which I want much more to think of to-night as the place which probably is quite new to scores and hundreds out of,

I suppose, the more than two thousand that we are. I wish particularly to speak to the many young men and young women who are here. I am not young in years ; I must be amongst the few oldest people in this tent. But young life is a long-lasting thing in man. A young life may beat within an old breast, and I think it usually does, at least a life young enough to feel with, to have some insight into, and to long to be even the least help to, the young men and the young women who want to possess their possessions and to use them for the Lord Jesus Christ.

Shall I illustrate by an incident what it is to possess possessions unpossessed before? I happen to know for certain the matters I am going to mention. Long years ago there was left a widow whose husband was a merchant in Manila ; he died on a business voyage, and was buried by an uncle of mine, who was then chaplain at Singapore. My uncle came to know the widow *à propos* of the burial, and told me this story. The lady, the widow, was left in very straitened circumstances at Manila. They had a little landed property in Australia, and she wrote to a business friend there to dispose of every bit of the ground, if he could. He sold it all, except one little plot that seemed so barren, and was so much out of the way for building, that nobody would buy. Well, so it was at first. She still owned the useless little plot of ground, rather against her will. But in 1850, two years later, they found gold in Australia, and in that little good-for-nothing field was discovered a gold mine. It was not a large one, but it was a gold mine, and it was enough, by its proceeds, to lift anxiety off the widow's heart. She told the story to my uncle, who told it to me. And so she had her possession all the time; the gold was every ounce of it under the ground all the time; but till she realized that it was there it was exactly to her as if it had not been. At last she possessed her possession, as a glad discovery, and it made a great difference to her life.

Is it not a parable, is it not an illustration? We possess the gold of the heavenly Ophir, all of it, in the Lord Jesus Christ. But it is possible to have a vast deal of the riches of that inexhaustible gold mine unrealized by our thoughts, untouched by our faith, unused in our life. What a glorious difference it may make when the discovery comes! Then we do not have a new Christ, and we do not have a new Gospel, and we do not have a new grace and glory, but we discover the ancient and the eternal in a way that makes it new to us, and we possess our possessions. Oh, the anxieties that are lifted off! Oh, the penury that is changed into spiritual rest and living ease! And oh, the joy that then comes to the trustee of the Master's heavenly wealth, as he tries to make use of it! For, after all, it is a trust for other souls.

Now, to illustrate a little further what I have said, I am going, after something of a conflict about it in my own mind, to take a line to-night which once, long years ago, I took beneath this tent. I am going to give you a personal experience of my own, to tell you the story of how I came to be a "Keswicker" at all. It has been a difficulty, it has been a struggle, to know whether it was quite right. When a man talks about himself there are many sorts of risks. It may do him serious harm if it is not done in the Lord. It may do others harm, in more ways than one. It may conceivably prejudice them against the truth. Or it may fix their minds so much on a human experience that they may not see simply the truth of Christ, for which alone it is told. But I have earnestly prayed that, in His mercy, this short and simple account may do good and not harm, and may set, not the bond-servant, who does not deserve to be mentioned, but his Master, before his dear friends in God. Listen to Onesimus, but look at Philemon all the time.

I first take you back just fifty-two years, to the time when I began to understand and possess some of the possessions which Keswick loves to show us the way to. In the year 1867, at twenty-five, my mother led me to the Lord Jesus Christ. I had taken my degree at Cambridge. I had a good post as a form-master in a great public school. I was very well satisfied with life. To a certain extent, with all sorts of internal contradictions to the feeling, I was fairly satisfied with myself. And God in His great mercy had kept me from what would be called wrong life, though not from a world of evil within. Then, one quiet day, I know not in the least how, nor shall know in this life, there came on me conviction of sin, in its old-fashioned form, a sight of how richly I deserved the wrath of God and banishment from Him for ever, for I had kept Him out of my heart. With almost a fire in my brain I went to my mother. I will not dwell upon her holy memory. Enough to say that she led me with God-given wisdom to the feet of Jesus, and as by spirit-sight I saw the Lamb upon the Cross of Calvary, and knew that He and only He stood between me and the second death. Then in due time I was ordained to the holy ministry—thank God, not before I had come to know Christ. And then I went on, at times with college duty, at times with parish duty; and in due time I was made Principal of a Theological Hall at Cambridge, with which I remained connected many years. I had been about four years there, living as the head of a religious institution, when I learned about certain possessions I had not possessed. I was on a visit with my family that autumn, 1884, at the house of a dearly loved relative in Scotland, near Linlithgow, a place where year after year the generous master and mistress had opened a great barn on their estate for what we may call a series of Keswick meetings. We, my family and I, were paying a visit to our friends, and the Convention was due to be held. Was I anxious to go? Not at all. I had been strongly prejudiced, much by my own fault, against the whole Keswick ideal. I thought it meant a doctrine of sinless perfection, which could only lead to an attitude in which the Christ of the atoning Cross seemed to cease to be necessary, and honestly I was afraid. But there was a great deal also of mixed motive, of jealousy and prejudice, in my mind. I wished to get away during the days of the Convention, but there was no opportunity to do this without breach of courtesy, and so I stayed; and, again as an act of courtesy, I went to the first meeting. It did not please me at all, and a severe conflict of thought and feeling followed upon it. Then there came the next night, and with some difficulty I made up my mind to go again. I still see the great barn, the thronging people, and myself sitting in the audience, by no means on the platform, listening to what might come, partly as the critic, but partly, I will admit, with a heart hungry for some gracious thing, if it was to be found. For I had begun to feel, after my years of converted life and ministerial work, guilty of discreditable failures in patience, and charity, and humbleness, and I know not what. I knew that I was not satisfied, and I knew that I ought to find what would satisfy me; but I did not expect to find it there. Two addresses were given that evening, the first by the late Mr. William Sloan, of Glasgow, a noble specimen of the Scottish business man, out and out for God. He spoke on the first chapter of Haggai, in words which I do not think I shall ever forget, taking to pieces the Christian life which is not satisfied, and piercing into the reasons why it is not satisfied, all more or less reducible to our letting the self-life intrude itself into the work of God; the man feeling himself, after all, well-nigh as important in Christian work as his Master. Somehow or other that address, under the Spirit's good guidance, pulled me to pieces with a second conviction of sin, the sin of the converted life, the sin of the professing Christian man. I may humbly say, thank God, that I was not a hypocrite. The Lord had showed me myself and Himself, in reality, as I have told you, long years before. But I had misread His promise, or read it so imperfectly that in deed and in truth I had a world of special sin to be convinced of that September night of 1884. And I remember, at the close of that address, feeling indescribably that it had been an even awful thing to go to that meeting. I was no longer the critic; the prejudices, the fears that there would be something, from the point of view of sacred orthodoxy (which *is* sacred), wrong and out of line, all vanished away. I knew that *this* was orthodox, the conviction of my sin.

Then the second address was given. The speaker was one whom I afterwards claimed, and claim still, for our relation is the same, though he has gone above, as my beloved friend, Evan Hopkins, of blessed memory. He rose up, and delivered an address as characteristic as possible, luminous as the light, perfect in arrangement, simple in expression, but with all the power of spiritual conviction in it. It was one long ordered piling up of the promises of God to the soul that will do two things towards Him—surrender itself into His hands, and trust Him for His mighty victory within. I will not—I must not—time flies—remind you what were the texts of the infallible Word which he piled up. It was as if there were two great weights in my balance. One was down heavily on the ground, loaded with the sins of my converted life and its grievous secret or open failures. Into the other balance the speaker now put promise after promise, aimed precisely at this, not for the unconverted man flying for refuge to the city where the guilty shall be safe under the protection of the high-priest, but the promises to that same fugitive, now dwelling in the city of refuge, who is starving there, and wretched, and miserable, because of himself. And as these promises were recited, grace enabled me to take them as meant, not to take them as read, but to take them as meant; to realize that they were meant to act; that I was to step on them with both feet, and to see if they did not bear. And so, in the great mercy of God, before I left that barn meeting, two consciousnesses had come in upon me. One was that I was in the hands of an absolute Master, so grasping and fettering me that I should have no interests outside His, seek no gain, or praise, or whatever it was, except for Him; that I was an illustration of the words of the ancient moralist, Aristotle, describing his theory of human slavery: "The slave is but a part of his master, he exists but for his master, he has no interests of his own, and yet he is, as it were, a limb of his master, separate yet living with his life."

So I went out of that meeting, back to the hospitable house where we were staying. I recollect, as I walked up the stairs to my room for the night, the consciousness with which I knew, on the one hand, that I was the absolute bond-slave of a sovereign and irresponsible Master, on the other hand that I had found a Friend and Liberator, a Helper, a Deliverer, a "goodness and a fortress," who would, so long and so much as I used Him, make me more than conqueror over the oldest temptation, over the most inveterate subtlety of the approach and invitation of evil, so as to teach even me how to walk and to please God. In the meeting of the next night I felt constrained to put pride into the pocket; to rise and say before all the people how the last night had been a great blessing to my soul.

Then in due time I had to go back to my responsible work at Cambridge. I knew there was in front of me a very difficult, laborious, perplexing term, with grave problems regarding movements of Christian life in Cambridge. And I was naturally a restless, impatient, and somewhat nervous being. But I recollect two things about that term. First, that, by a power certainly not my own, I was able to meet every threatened difficulty with a quiet mind, which was half the victory beforehand. Then, what was the very opposite to my nature, when I was hard at work in my study, and an unlooked-for knock at the door came—instead of the old thrill and twist of impatience, there was the pleasure the swimmer feels in climbing a wave, because it gives him a free sense of the lift of the water, and the delight at once of action and of rest. These things now did not put me out. I possessed my possession. A Christ submitted to, a Christ trusted, a Christ used, made life a different thing.

All this was thirty-five years ago, dear friends in Christ, before a great many of you were born ; but it is to me as if yesterday. What have I to say as to the time since then ? Has it been unbroken victory, has it been unbroken rest ? No. By whose fault ? Never the Master's. Every day and every hour He has been as full of help as ever, He has been as close at hand as ever. But did I never get indolent in the use of His helps to keeping awake ? Did I never let myself get slack about regular prayer, when there was no excuse for slackness ? Did I never let myself get careless over search of the Bible ? Did I never let myself get indifferent about little bits of unpretending duty? Inevitably then something seemed as if it paralysed the fingers that were to use the Lord. And the Lord, unused, humbled the man again and again, by letting him feel what it would all be again if he did not possess his possessions and use what he possessed. But I know this well, that to this day, through these long years, with a Church and a world changed, with my life changed, as many a joy and many a sorrow has come over it, while God has often broken up the ground under my feet and clouded the sky above my head, and has put me to some of the greatest tests that human loss can bring, while also crowning me with mercies—all I can say is that, just as the old secret is used, the surrender of the spirit to the Lord, the same delightful results are assured, because He is the same. There is still a rest and a power for the soul, which means nothing less than this wonderful Christ, whom I saw in conversion, and who is indeed Christ for me now, in this after-blessing, as I ought to have seen Him from the first. Christ is still in me to make the weak strong, to make the easily defeated Christian conqueror, through Him that loved us.

So I lay this before you. I have ventured thus, so to speak, to bare my breast—not an easy thing for an Englishman to do—to bare the breast of my experience before you, in the humble hope that, with all the boundless differences between one life and another all round, there will be enough in what I have told to come home to you, as to human hearts that have a sight of God, and to help you to a recollection of the treasures and the wealth that are laid up for us in the Lord Christ Jesus, to be won, to be used, freely, not by laborious efforts and meritorious deservings. The plan of the Gospel is that the divine acceptance is to come first, and the glad, happy service is to follow out of that, until the goal is reached above. I hope my story may come home, near enough to the common element in our human hearts, to remind you that we are meant to live as those who are spiritually rich, to spend our wealth freely for the real needs of our own lives in purity and in holy peace, and then, heart and soul, to use it for the needs of others. Yes, we will let our own experience of the Lord be serviceable to other hearts, whether by His enabling us to live a life which will make things brighter for them, though we may never say a word to them, or by His giving us just the tact which experienee of what Christ is gives:

the skill to speak in humbleness and sympathy, yet with truth and directness, to other hearts. So I, in His dear name, invite to-night to His feet and to His heart whosoever here has not yet dug that part of the ground of our hid treasure which has under it the conquering power of a trusted Christ, used by the weak and helpless soul which, simply trusting for its liberty and its victory, comes to Him as to its Master. You will find it good to belong, absolutely to belong :

> I love, I love my Master,
> I will not go out free ;
> For He is my Redeemer,
> He paid the price for me.

You will be like that happy being in the Mosaic law who had found absolute possession by a good man so delightful, that when the seven years of temporary servitude were over he said, " I love thee ; I will be thy slave for ever." And lo ! at once the awl was driven through his ear to the house-door, to signify perpetual obedience and perpetual belonging to the home. Yes, you will find it good, taken by itself, to say the " I will " of an out-and-out submission to the Lord. But then, use the

Lord you have submitted to as your possession, and you will find victories that will astonish yourself over that old temptation which you have fought so often, and mean to fight again, but which seems as strong as ever. It may be that misery of temper; it may be that unforgiven injury which you cannot forget; it may be that habit, you know hardly how to define it, but which you know keeps your soul down; it may be some deep secret sin which you would be shocked for your most intimate friend to guess, yet it seems to come up like an earthquake from beneath, and to shake the whole structure of your soul. You will find that all this shall be stilled and subdued, and you shall have liberty, victory, and a happy, perpetual, upward growth, using Him who is in this wonderful sense your possession.

And you will find that you are dealing with a Lord who is immeasurably ready to respond. We have every reason to trust Him who has cared for us so much that He stooped from the Throne to the cradle, from the cradle to the Cross, and thence to the grave through an unfathomable death, simply that you and I might live. We will not be afraid of His slavery, and we will be perfectly confident not merely of His power, but of His delighted willingness, to be our liberator. So be it, for each and all of these Thy tried ones, Lord Jesus Christ.

IV.

Our dear-bought Body and its Use.

IN 1 Cor. vi. 20, it is thus written: "Ye are bought with a price; therefore glorify God in your body."

I would begin by calling attention to the point where, in this verse, my quotation ends. If we have our Authorized Version before us we shall see, as we probably know, that the verse goes on, "and in your spirit, which are God's." Those words are divinely true. But it is fairly certain, as a matter of literary enquiry, that the actual words written by St. Paul stopped at "body." Accordingly you will find in the Revised Version, whose workers had fuller evidence before them as to the original words, that we read only, "therefore glorify God in your body." Probably, very early in Christian history, some devout and loving student of the Word wrote into his copy, as a note, what his heart dictated to him as so supremely true—that the spirit, as well as the body, must be used to glorify the Lord, and then those words, in subsequent copies, may have passed into the text. There are just a few such passages in our blessed Scriptures. Let us remember one happy fact about them; there is not one which in the least degree goes off the lines of the eternal truth, or should disturb for a moment the Christian's faith in the Written Word. But here and there, meanwhile, an interesting lesson can be drawn when we come to find the slight difference which appears to exist between a verse as we have it in a version in our own tongue, and that verse as it came first from the pen of the apostle; and this verse beyond reasonable doubt lends itself to such a lesson.

"Ye are bought with a price: therefore glorify God in your body." We may paraphrase it thus: "You have been bought dear; you, *with all your physical faculties*, are purchased property, bought so dear that it is all-important to the Purchaser that He should have His purchase in full condition and fit for full use." The first inference from that is that you, the purchased property, being a living, willing, loving being, must respond to the Purchaser, and see to it on your side that, by His grace but through your will, the purchased property is being continually delivered over to the Purchaser, as it should be, for His use.

I have taken this short portion of the Word, feeling that no text could well be more familiar, and no lesson could be more obvious, than what I think it has been laid on me to draw from it, to a meeting in the Keswick tent. But if my experience is the least like that of my friends in Christ, it is often the obvious and the familiar that we most need to take again and, as it were, stand back from and look at anew. A further thought in my mind is this, as it was last night—that there are many here undoubtedly this morning, (particularly young brethren and sisters, who are very much upon my heart, with their glorious possibilities), who are now for the first time visitors to the Convention. And if I speak with thought directed to them I do not think that to my other friends here present it will be an unwelcome thing that we should bend our heart and prayer very specially to-day, and through this week, upon those who are rising to take the place of us veterans in the Lord's army. Some of us, I for one, cannot be here much longer, in the order of nature. We know in any case that there is this perpetual need of a reinforcement moving up to the front, well-trained and ready, sure to find its call to meet the world, the flesh, and the devil, in the front rank, with testimony to a trusted Christ and His power, in and through the life that has begun its fuller course with a fuller surrender to Him.

Continuing these few thoughts by way of preface, there comes to me one further word to say, as suggested by the verses read by our honoured chairman, from the first chapter of the short book of Haggai. That passage tells how things all went wrong in the city while the temple remained unrestored, how blessing was deferred upon the common interests of life till God had been put into the first place, in the most visible and manifest way in which they could do it. I think that passage will have come home to all our hearts, and to none more than my own.

For on the occasion that I ventured to speak of last night, which first drew me into the line of Keswick thought and life, and made me humbly glad to be a Keswick disciple—on that occasion, in that barn in Scotland so long ago, this passage, as I said last night, was what "took me to pieces," in the detection, the unveiling to my own soul and conscience, of the grievous lackings in the spiritual life within, and how greatly they were due to letting self take the Master's place in work which seemed to be for Him. As I welcome again the solemn and searching words, I trust that they may be a new message to myself, who need them and shall need them to the very end; and that for us all, with every lesson God gives us in a positive and uplifting way in Keswick this week, they may live, so to speak, at the back of our thoughts, reminding us of the supreme practical importance, for life and happy usefulness, of letting the Lord have His proper place without mistake.

Now I come to the passage I have read. I will begin at the end and ask why it is that the apostle emphasizes and underlines the thought of *the body.* "Therefore glorify God in your body." We know how much deeper, naturally, is the doctrine of the spirit than the doctrine of the body, so much so that we may say that the body exists for the spirit, as its vehicle, as its tool. Yes, but it is just because of the enormous and vital importance, to the spirit, of the body, in the living out of human life as God has put us into this world to live it, that the Bible makes so very much of the body. You know that it does so in many another passage. You remember Romans xii. 1: "I beseech you, by the mercies of God, that ye present *your bodies* a living sacrifice." There is another very searching and solemn passage in 2 Cor. v.: "We must all appear before the judgment-seat of Christ"—His servants must appear before what we may call His domestic judgment-seat, to hear what the Master of the family thinks, not of the outside world, but of the family, as they have behaved, one by one—"that we may receive the things done *through the body.*" That is the literal rendering of St. Paul's words, which you will find in the margin of the Revised Bible;

"That we may receive the things done *through the body*"; a rendering which I wish with all my heart had been put into the translation itself, because it means so much. He will want to know *how we have used our bodies*. He will want to know what has been the spirit's action, not in the abstract, but *through the body*. When He comes, and when one and another of His servants appear before Him (to change the metaphor) with what they have won with their talents—and one of the great talents is the body—when they hear what the Master thinks on that matter, may His word to us be, "Well done, good and faithful."

I will dwell a little more upon this presently, upon the immense importance, from every side in our Christian life, of the things done *through* the body. For the moment, however, I leave that, and now come to the first great word of the text: "Ye are bought with a price," or, as we may paraphrase it, "You have been bought dear." I want to lay that all-familiar word, "bought," fresh upon my own heart and upon yours this morning. We are every one of us a purchased article for which an immense price has been given. I need not labour out that point to the Bible lovers and seekers after Christ that, thank God, the congregation of this tent are. But while we do not labour it out, or talk of it as a thing which is to be elaborately proved, let us say it out to each one of us again, that each one is a purchased article, acquired by a Possessor at an immense price. The thought of this purchasing and possessing at a price, you know, runs through the Word of God, and it comes out now and then, as here, in articulate intensity. "Ye were not bought," says St. Peter, "with corruptible things, as silver and gold, but with the precious blood of Christ, as of a lamb without blemish." And Rev. v. opens to us a vision of the glorified, and lets us catch the articulate accents of their song; and there, in the land of life eternal, where death has long been dead and the grave long buried, they never cease to sing about that death, and to remind the Prince of Life upon the throne before them, to whom their whole being goes out in worship, to whom their whole being is one song, that He once, to acquire them as His own, died a sanguinary death. "Thou art worthy, for Thou wast slain, and hast *redeemed us* unto God by Thy blood."

We know that the shedding of that most sacred blood was, after all, only the outward and visible sign of an immeasurable, invisible reality—the giving by the incarnate God of Himself in sacrifice, that you and I through that death might live. We shall never know, not even, I think, in heaven (for surely it can be understood only upon the throne) all that that death was. Think of the outward agonies of the sacred and perfect Body, whose very perfection must have made it capable of pain in an inconceivable degree. But remember not only the agonies of the body, but the infinite sufferings of the Lord's human soul under the outrage, and insult, and blaspheming raillery around Him. The bodily tortures were not the depth of the woe; they were the Atlantic waves upon the surface. Even the pangs of feeling under hideous insult were not the depth. The miles of depth, in the dark below the waves, which God only can fathom, are indicated in that cry out of the supernatural night that settled down over Him: "My God, why hast Thou forsaken me?" Remember, that was the price paid. *He gave Himself for us*, and the Self was that unspeakably wonderful Lord Jesus Christ, the Son of the eternal Father, the Son of the mortal mother—Incarnate God.

> " Forbid it, Lord, that I should boast,
> Save in the death of Christ my God :
> All the vain things that charm me most,
> I sacrifice them to His blood."

This Blood means that unfathomable death, which assuredly would not have been died if our need had not been inexpressibly great, and only to be met so.

May I pause for a moment to use here once again what in our smaller but much blest gatherings last year I remember venturing to use—an illustration as to the Lord's death, and how it teaches us what sin in its evil and its ghastly peril is, as to which even the Christian world often takes such light views to-day? That dreadful saying, "The modern man does not worry much about his sins," I am afraid embodies an immense deal of thought not only in the openly and frankly unbelieving world, but in many circles of the Church. There exists widely a low view of sin, and a constant forgetting that man needs not only to be relieved of sorrow, and to be cheered in death, and to be guided in duty, but to be saved from the "second death," and to be saved from the awful mischief and malady of sin now. My illustration is this. Suppose I am unwell, feeling myself ill enough to send for my doctor, but not thinking my case particularly serious. But ere long I sink into unconsciousness, for there is more the matter than I thought. The unconscious state lasts, as such states do sometimes, a long time, two or three days. When I wake up I am conscious that a new presence is in my room. There is my old friend and doctor; there is a trained nurse at my side. But there is somebody else in the room. I have not the least idea of his identity, and I whisper to the nurse, "Who is that?" She whispers back to me the name of the greatest specialist in the United Kingdom for a certain very serious disease indeed. I know that his home is hundreds of miles from mine, and I know that he must have been sent for urgently over the long journey, and here he is at my side. I want no logical argument now to prove to me that I have been very ill. The eminence of the doctor is abundant evidence of the imminence of the disease. I have been very near death, or he would not be in the room at all. And now, here are we men and women, made in the image of God, and that image by man's sin broken, hopelessly broken; how in the world is it to be restored? We are sick unto death of a malady whose end is not the first death, but the second, the death that cannot die. And, lo, we are led to "a green hill far away, outside a city wall," and we see there a shockingly outraged Human Form expiring under black darkness on a cross, a gibbet, upon that hill, and we hear from the lips of that Victim of judicial murder (as it is, on one side), that cry of well-nigh despair: "My God" (the one note not of despair in it is "My"), "my God, why hast Thou forsaken me?" We wonder what it means, and some divine informant comes and tells us: "That is God, made Man, dying because you had sinned." Think then what my sin must have been, think what sin must be, think what in the Eternal Light its blackness seems. As an American evangelist, I believe, boldly put it, "If we could see sin's blackness, it would make a black mark upon a lump of coal!" We cannot know it properly, we cannot realize it; but let us all the more think of what is said about it, and how it is revealed not by the terrors of an unredeemed future but by the glory of the Cross. That is the price paid that you and I might be saved. The Lord died to save us, to rescue us from a peril so great in His view as to justify that supreme and unfathomed agony, for our salvation.

But I want you to think another thought about that sacrifice—that it was *purchase* as well as rescue. Rescue can be thought of entirely apart from appropriation. A strong swimmer may have the great joy of saving from the deep a brother being's life, but without the smallest intention, or duty, to take thereupon that being to be supported by his means and in his home. Rescue is one thing, and the Lord indeed suffered to effect it. But the point is this—He loved us so well that He was not content to *save*; He must also *have*. Therefore the saving was appropriation. The Passion was ransom also; its result was His acquisition of a complete ownership over the souls He saved. I ask you to remember that this is not only a theoretical truth. It brings with it this mighty bond; it claims from every one of us a willing surrender to such a possessor, for we are every one of us acquired at so illimitable a price. It would be scandalous that this Purchaser should not have the purchase. And as we are not inanimate articles, but beings made in the image of God, with moral will, and love, and thought, it is for us to recognize, and so far to satisfy, the claim by saying "*Yes*" to the Lord, as to the rightness of His possessing us, as to the criminal wrongness of our retaining anything out of His hard-won property.

But the other point I ask you to remember is the *love* of it. Why did the Lord so desire to have us? Was it just that He might tyrannize over us, and enjoy possession, as a tyrant might, by doing what he likes, including the infliction of great injuries on his slave? No; the Lord wanted to have us absolutely, because He loved us, and coveted us, and desired us, unspeakably. It was like the merchantman seeking the pearl, the secreted, goodly pearl. It was His love of the human soul, His desire for the work of His own hands, His tender affection for the race that He had taken into oneness with Himself when He let Himself be born at Bethlehem a real human Babe—it was that which made the Lord covet the complete possession of you and me. The more we know ourselves, the more the wonder is. Oh, how canst Thou care so much for me? How canst Thou not only compassionate but *like to have me?* But here is the fact that "He gave Himself for us, that He might purchase to Himself," as St. Paul says to Titus, "a peculiar people," that is to say, as you know, in the old meaning of the word "peculiar," *a possession people,* a people of His very own. Think of the love of it, and let that love which showed itself in the dying of that death to redeem be ever, in the depth of our souls and in the heart of our lives, the supreme motive as we listen to a text like this. "Now," says St. Paul, in the text, "put it into practice thus: *glorify God in your body.*"

I said that we would think a little further, towards the end, about the body. Dear friends, there are dark sides to the truth of the body, which make the Bible sometimes speak about the body sternly. "I keep under my body, I keep it in subjection," says the great apostle. In his own Greek words it is literally: "I drag it about as a slave." But this is only part of the truth about the body, though it is a side of truth that we have all to remember. You, dear young men, with whom I still feel myself so much one, you know it. But all the more, what you want to be reminded of is just this: it is your Purchaser's and Redeemer's will that your bodily life should be clean all through. And it is your Purchaser's and Redeemer's promise, if you will use Him as your trusted Christ, that it shall be, and shall be kept, clean all through. It is a voice from beneath which says, "Young manhood must have its taste of sin, because it is manhood." Not so, a hundred times. The Lord says that He is able to keep you from falling, and He can, and He does.

I quoted in private, after my address last night, to two young men friends who were good enough to speak to me about what had been said—I quoted words said, to me here, perhaps thirty years ago, by a true-hearted lay Christian who was with us, words also mentioned by me at Crosthwaite Church on Sunday evening. We were talking about young men's temptations. My friend said: " In my young manhood I was greatly tempted " (it was a very full young manhood in his case, and the devil makes much use of that) " to go wrong, but God kept me clean all through, and I will tell you how. When the devil whispered, ' Sin is sweet; and others do it; why not you ? ' something moved me always to shut my eyes, and say to my own heart the two words, ' JESUS CHRIST.' And as I pronounced the Name the temptation seemed dead under my feet, and the enemy, who did not fear me, but who desperately fears my Lord—he had fled." Whether it be such dark temptations, or the easy-going temptations of indolent habits, careless, self-disrespectful habits, in secret, or anyhow, remember that two things are true—He calls you to give them up, and He can enable you to give them up, all round.

But, then, I want to remind you most of the positive side of the truth about the body—the vast importance of its being, by God's grace, kept clean, and in the highest sense *fit*, at whatever age and in whatever state of health, *fit for God's use.* How grandly useful for God it is meant to be! The fact is as plain as the midday sun that it is through the body, and practically through the body only, that we are always telling on one another. How am I trying to help you to-day? Here is my soul and spirit; but suppose there was nothing of me but my soul and spirit in this tent, I do not think my presence would make much difference to any one. But the Lord sends me here as a spirit *embodied*, with lungs, and with lips, and with tongue, with brain, with general bodily faculties, able to stand up before you on my feet, to open my book with my hands, to meet your eyes with mine. It is *through the body* that I am attempting to serve you now. So it is with us all, all day long. We are telling upon one another through the lips of our body as we talk; through the eyes of our body, the expression of our face, as we look; through the things we do with our hands, even to the grasp of a hand, which may be a magnetic means of touch between spirit and spirit. It is through this, that, and the other bodily organ that you and I are continually living, not the isolated life which we may conceive a spirit might live, but the life that tells all round upon one another, and which is meant to be for the glory of God. Therefore most urgently necessary it is that we should recollect the importance, the sacredness, the divine usableness, of these familiar things, our bodies, and present them as living sacrifices to Him who gave the supreme living Sacrifice for us, to make us His own possession.

I would ask you to remember, next, that this recollection of the duty and the privilege of a God-glorifying use of the body is the path not only of usefulness but of happiness. The life which is so true to the Lord in the spirit, that in the body it is true to His will of purity, and truth, and untiring kindness, going out from self to others in that noble sense of love which a philosopher long ago laid down as "that which finds its happiness in the good of another"—that life is the straight path to happiness and brightness for the man or the woman who lives it. I have sometimes illustrated it, in my pastoral talks in my diocese, particularly when confirming dear young people there. Speaking, of course, with absolute homeliness to them, I have illustrated it by the story, told me by a clergyman on the Tyne, of a conversion in his parish, which he heard of through the big lad's mother. The mother said: "You know, I am a widow and not very strong, and my oldest boy goes out to work every day, close to home, and comes in to dinner. He used, when he came in to dinner, if I had not got it quite ready, to turn round and abuse me. But you know, there was that Mission in the parish, and somebody persuaded him to go, and somehow or other God got hold of him; and now he still goes out to work, and he still comes in to dinner, and still I am not always able to have it ready; but now he looks at me, ever so bright, and he says, 'Mother, shall I help get it ready?'" Now God was in those words. They were not about angels, and archangels, and the company of heaven; they were about *dinner* and *mother*. But God was in them, and the point that I make of them often is this: *When was that lad happiest?* When he was thinking only of his own miserable self, and abusing his mother for not getting dinner ready sooner? or when he was making his mother's heart sing? You cannot make other people's hearts sing without getting some of the song into your own. That is true all round the true life, sooner or later, more or less, and in God's goodness it shall be ***more***. That is what will be true for every life which, having in spirit come to Jesus, now makes the body, the external life which tells on others, a willing and living sacrifice to the supreme Sacrifice Himself. That life is sunny as it never was before; there is a song in it that never sounded there before, and which is an echo of the song of heaven, but perfectly real on earth.

I draw now to a close, but with the earnest hope that out of this great, this splendid gathering, which makes the hearts of us old "Keswickers" so glad, may go a great contribution of glory to God. That is what we come up here for, is it not? We come, no doubt, to get mercies for our own souls; no doubt, as to many a beloved heart in this tent, to find in Christ Jesus the one possible solace for great and bitter griefs. At this tremendous time there is sure to be a large sprinkling of broken hearts in the tent this morning. And what I would pray for is that these broken hearts may realize for one thing that they have to do with a once broken-hearted God. We Christians have that unique and marvellous privilege among men, that we worship a once broken-hearted God. He is now in infinite felicity; He has suffered, and that is past. But, as a noble French proverb says, "*To have suffered* endures for ever." He will never forget it; and the blessed in heaven will never let Him forget it: "Thou wast slain." But now, for us all, the great thing is to offer to Him the living, willing, sacrifice of self at the heart, involving that of the body on the surface, to be what He would like, so far as we can gather it, at His feet, out of His Word; to be natural people, human people, companionable people, and yet people whose "life is hid with Christ in God," and the surface of whose life is by His grace, therefore, kept true in cleanness, in truthfulness, in kindness always, for Him. So by grace it shall be. And now we will, before we close, in one of our sweetest, deepest, truest hymns, gather up some of these thoughts of the glorious results of believing surrender, not merely of the secrecies of our being, but of the bodily activities and externals of it, to the Lord Jesus Christ. Let us sing the hymn (No. 70):

"Make me a captive, Lord,
And then I shall be free;
Force me to render up my sword,
And I shall conqueror be."

V.

Liberty for Bondservice.

IN Gal. v. 13 we read : " Brethren, ye have been called unto liberty ; only use not liberty for an occasion to the flesh, but by love serve one another."

One or two syllables may be altered in the wording of this verse to bring it nearer in modern speech. We may paraphrase somewhat thus : " You have been called " (a word which, with St. Paul, means almost precisely what we commonly mean by the great word *converted ;* not a mere invitation, but the effectual result of the invitation of God to the soul to " turn round " to Him, with all that it shall mean) " you have been converted, on terms of liberty." That is to say, He designed in your conversion that you should be free, free in thought, and love, and will. He made you free from the curse of the law, from the burden of the doom of sin hovering and haunting ; letting you know, under the great and eternal " new covenant," that your sins and your iniquities He remembereth, because of Christ, no more. A great liberty !

And then also, He willed you to be free from the bondage of victorious sin within, to find more than victory, through the trusted Christ, dwelling in your heart, and making it the scene of the putting forth of His own wonderful and living power against evil and for good. So that, in the terms of the other limb of the eternal "new covenant," He has "put His law into your mind and written it on your heart," and you are free from the bondage of victorious sin within. You walk in the liberty of a holy acceptance, and in the liberty of a holy, willing, conformity to the will of God in Jesus Christ our Lord. You find and feel in your life now that "religion is a great success."

I quote those last words; I quote them from five-and-thirty years ago, when I heard them said in a little testimony-meeting of young men at Cambridge, by one of the most reserved and reticent men I have ever known. He had been, before the blessing which he undoubtedly then received, an almost inaccessible person, with a shut-up nature, with a powerful mind, working in a steadfast and isolated life. But God found him, and gave him the liberty of the knowledge of pardon and peace, and the liberty of deliverance from the tyranny of self. There soon afterwards occurred, as I have said, a testimony-meeting, and others were there who gave glad testimony, some not in few words, to what the Lord had done for them. But this man, evidently with a great effort, said just this: "I have found at last that religion is a great success." We who knew him could interpret the eloquence of those simple words. He found he had been called "on terms of liberty," as against the anxious struggle to be religious, the anxious struggle to win God's favour and peace, the anxious struggle to overcome temptations in the name of his own powerful will, in conflict with something more powerful still—the threefold stress of the world, the flesh, and the devil. His conscience was now free, in pardon and peace. And his will was free, in the surrender he had made to the Lord Jesus Christ, to be treated in His way.

We may then, once more, retranslate the beginning of the verse: "You were converted upon terms of liberty." And you are meant to realize your liberty, and to be glad of it;

not to treat it as a thing to be spoken of only with doubtful terms and large reserves. You have found that the Gospel means *great things* in pardon, and *great things* in purifying power. And you are meant to have a great sense of liberation, through this wonderful promotion into the liberty of the children of God. St. Paul reminds the Galatians that it was so with them. He had had a great deal of trouble over teachings of another sort that had crept in amongst them, and that would drag them back, if that was possible, to the bondage of the old days. The Epistle to the Galatians was the inspired message of the Master through His messenger, to dispel the delusion that there could ever be a religiousness more devout, that there could ever be a worship more deep, that there could ever be a reverence more humble, than that which is learned by the liberated soul at the foot of the Cross, receiving the breath and fire of Pentecost which for us falls there. So one message from this text this evening to you and to me is that we should indeed covet and love our liberty greatly, that we should not be entangled with yokes of bondage, that we should look steadfastly and afresh into the glorious largeness of the apostolic Gospel, which embodies itself in those wonderful words of the "new covenant," given first through Jeremiah (in that great passage in his thirty-first chapter), and enunciated and sealed by the Lord when He said, as He founded His sacred Communion, "This cup is the new covenant in my blood." We are to remember that under that covenant our sins and iniquities are remembered no more, not because we have obeyed, but *that we may obey, in peace.* And then we have the promise of the willing Lord that, as to the restoration and the renovation of our souls and wills into harmony with God, He will delight to do it, if we spread the heart out in humble submissiveness before Him. He will take the pen, and write His will upon the heart, and put His law into it. In other words, He will see to it, as He reigns within, that He adjusts our will to His, and then it will move in liberty indeed.

But then, what has St. Paul to say at the close of this golden passage? "Do not use your liberty for an occasion to the flesh." If we want to interpret, in the shortest and homeliest way, the meaning of the Pauline word, "the flesh," I do not think we can do better than say that it practically means *the self*, in the sense of the life of self-love, self-assertion, self-will. It is a deep word, as we trace the use of it, taught by the Holy Spirit, in the writings of St. Paul. So here he says, in effect, do not use your freedom as an opportunity for self. Do not think your spiritual liberty is given you to walk away with and enjoy it by yourself. Do not think for one moment that it is meant to put you on a pedestal, to make you think that you are better than other people. Do not think that it is to isolate your sympathies, and take you away from all possible fellowship with other souls. Use it for the very opposite purpose. "By love"—which is nothing if it is not that which goes out of self—"by love serve one another." So says our English. "*Slave for one another*," says St. Paul's Greek. Just realize that you *belong to other people* because you belong to the Lord. All that He has given, in the peace of justifying acceptance, and in the peace of liberation from victorious sin within, is to be used for others. Spend it as those should spend it who know and belong to the wonderful Saviour who sealed the covenant with His *self-sacrificed* blood. Spend it and use it as those should do who belong to other people. There is no dear Christian life in this hall to-night but is bound, delightfully bound, bound by the cords of heavenly love, to use the spiritual life unselfishly. You are to receive it without a doubt, to rejoice in it with an invigorating happiness, to be personally, so far as these great reasons can ensure it, a happy Christian, happy whether the sunshine of the present shines around you, or whether time, change, and loss, cover you with a cloud. Whether it be under a sunny or a shadowed sky, you are meant to be personally happy, even as you may hear a lark singing equally brightly—as how often I have done!—over meadows shining and smiling with unclouded summer, or over dreary places under a frowning heaven. You are meant to be happy and to enjoy your happiness. But then you are meant to use what you enjoy, and to enjoy it all the better for using it, for other people. Whatever God has taught you in your liberty, it is something that you can use for other people. He has taught you how earthly happiness gains wonderfully by this spiritual liberty, as flowers gain in beauty and expansion under the sun. That is something to help other people with. Then He has taught you that, under an agonizing grief, He really and wonderfully can get so near to you that you feel it possible, because of what that helps you to do for other people, gladly to say, " Blessed be the name of the Lord." *There* is something in which you can use the (not man-won but God-given) liberty for other people.

So we remember this as one of the great laws of the Christian life, without which it is out of gear—and what is out of gear is apt to run with friction and trouble. We remember that we are called to a life free, and wonderfully happy and cheered within; but a life which is to be spent upon willing slavery to other people; a life in which we begin each day not with the idea of, " How much comfort and pleasure for myself, or how much gain and advantage for myself, can I get out of the day?"

but, " How delightful if the Lord should enable me to-day to make things brighter, temporally, or spiritually, or both, for other people ! "—to help some maimed folks over stiles, to say a word in season to some tired hearts, to make the air brighter and sweeter in a home, because of the liberty and joy of the Lord in a member of that home, perhaps the head of it, or perhaps the youngest member of it. If we only remember that this is the wonderful and noble privilege to which we are called as liberated Christians, then we shall be corresponding to the ideal of the Gospel, we shall be corresponding to the will of the Lord. It will be because His law has been written by His pen upon that strange surface, on which He knows how to write—our hearts.

Remember that this is quite certain, in a deep sense, and also in a true, natural and human sense, this sure and increasing happiness of the free being which lives to serve.

They tell us—it is one of the doctrines of what is known as the new psychology—that self, that is, *personality*, is not *born*, but *made* by the contacts and relationships of life. I venture to think that the phrase, though undoubtedly written, where I read it lately, by a very clever person, was not very accurate, and that what was meant was not the personality but the shape, the *character*, which the personality comes to take. But the thought was this—that, normally speaking, it is inconceivable that an isolated personality should come to its best, should " realize itself " without contact with others. And this statement of the results of acute observation upon the realities of ordinary human life, seems to me to have a profound correspondence to the Gospel ideal which was set by the supreme experience of the Lord, when He refused to live isolated upon the throne of uncreated bliss, but came into contact with mortal personalities as their self-sacrificing Redeemer. For thereby—I say it with profound reverence—He has won to all eternity a joy which, in the nature of things, He would otherwise have foregone. For had He not so done, He could not have had that joy, eternal as the heavens, which will be His when the lives of the innumerable nations of the blessed will always be singing their thanks to Him. I take it, the music of Heaven will largely consist in the being, and the work, and the service, and the loving energies, of the Blessed; and that music will all converge upon this: "Thou art worthy; for Thou wast slain, and hast redeemed us unto God." That "joy set before Him" is what actuated *the Supreme Believer,* as the Epistle to the Hebrews calls Him, practically, in the twelfth chapter and the second verse. (For that is really the meaning of the phrase, "author and finisher of faith." Please strike the word "*our*" out of that verse. In both our English Versions it is printed in italics, to mark it as an insertion; and it is, I dare to say, a mistaken insertion.) "Looking unto Jesus, the author and finisher of faith," the Supreme Believer, who lived, who suffered, who overcame, by that boundless *trust, through the dark,* in His Father, which carried Him through Gethsemane and Golgotha. And He did it "for the joy set before Him"—not a selfish joy, though a personal one, but the joy of being for ever our Saviour, loved by us as such; and the joy too of seeing something of His character reproduced in liberated but slaving people, who delight to give themselves, like Him, fo others.

So I leave the text upon your hearts. We are called to liberty—and dear Keswick exists very largely to remind us that we are so called; to liberty from condemnation because of Christ for us; to liberty from bondage to victorious sin within because of Christ in us; but called to liberty that we may freely *slave*, that we may willingly give ourselves for others, and thereby may cultivate for our own personality a development into pure, personal, unselfish gladness, the Lord making us, in His mercy, causes of help and joy to other people, not less gladly because it is at cost to ourselves. And so may He carry whatever has been His own Word to-night home to each one of us, to the glory of His Name, to the good of His Church, and to the good and gladness of each Christian soul itself.

VI.

The Abiding Presence.

I READ to you one of the most familiar of the Gospel utterances of our Lord. In the last words of St. Matthew's Gospel, as in our Authorized, so in our Revised Version, the words stand: "I am with you alway, even unto the end of the world." But let us take the words fresh from the original, and render them almost *verbatim*: "I am with you all the days, even unto the consummation of the age." And if we may refine a little upon the grammar of the original, without dwelling upon the reason why, it is not too much to paraphrase the words: "I am with you all the days, *and all day long*, even unto the consummation of the age."

What I would do in these few minutes is not out of keeping with the special object of this assembly, special prayer for special needs. It is surely in deepest harmony with it, though the passage does not speak explicitly about prayer. For is not the very soul and animation of prayer connected vitally with the recollection of the immediate presence of the Lord whom we speak to? We need, again and again, to remember His promise of presence if, not only in our spiritual life generally, but in our life of prayer, we would grow and prosper. This solemn affirmation by the Master of His perpetual presence, not only vaguely spread over time, but put into its details, is surely timely for this sacred hour of prayer.

With that remembrance let me simply come to the words themselves. "*I am.*" He speaks in the accent of one who, while He was Man among men in His resurrection life, as much Man as ever with that company upon the hill in Galilee, probably the five hundred and more mentioned by St. Paul (1 Cor. xv. 6)—and the Lord Christ was as human as any one of them—still He speaks in the accents of one who is also eternal, above time. He does not say, "I will be," but "I am." It is an eternal present tense, irrespective of time and change as from our point of view. To the Lord it is just one way of saying that we may count upon His unalterable presence every day, every hour, every minute that we live.

Then I ask you to note the beautiful significance of the full original words: "I am with you *all the days*." How different days are from one another! Some are golden, some are gray, and some are black; some are warm and summerlike, others tend to freeze the very springs of hope and of cheer. There are immense differences between days, even in the most ordinary life, and under the most common circumstances, as our inner world touches at a thousand points the outer world, and feels the influences. Therefore, let us thank Him who said, in this wonderful way: "I am with you all the days, and I am with you"—if again I may touch upon the spiritual message through the detail of grammar—"*all the day long*." The Greek indicates not a *point*, but a *surface*; over the days, through them, from morning till night, from night till morning. He "will be the arm every morning." How often the hard worker, the anxious heart, feels the morning anything but a time of light and cheer! It is the place of outlook upon dreaded things not seldom. But He who is with you all the day long—from the morning, with its care, its heavy care, apart from Him; to the noon with its stress; to the afternoon with its frequent sense of weight and heaviness; to the evening with its fatigue—He knows all about it.

> "There is no secret sigh we breathe
> But meets His ear Divine.
>
> "He who has trod the thorny road
> Will share the small distress;
> The hand that bore the greater load
> Will not refuse the less."

The things that we can hardly express to an intimate friend, as well as the great things that stand out as the problems of life—this wonderful Lord knows them all. "I am with you."

Then let us remember that He is with us—this is one thought I would specially seek to leave with you—because He loves and likes to be there. Have we thought enough of that amazing indication of our Master's love, that He *likes* to be with us? There is no sign of love more sure, more tender, than the wish to be always together. Love is so felt towards you and me by our

Lord Jesus Christ. "He died for us," says the Apostle, "that we might live"—and not only that we might live, but that we might live—"*together with Him.*" His own prospect of eternity is, "that they whom Thou hast given Me be with Me where I am, that they may behold my glory." As we thought on a former occasion, such is His love that He is not content with *saving*. There must be *having* too. And not only *having*; for possession may be of a thing far off. There must also be *company*. He delights to have us with Him, and to be with us. Shall I ever forget a young and most beloved sufferer looking up to her mother's face, and saying, "Do you not only *love* me, but *like* me?" You see the point. We cannot like ourselves, when we know all that we can know about our poor hearts. But we do know that such as the Lord, not because we are lovable, but because He is love, that He likes the company of His people, He, the Mighty One before whom His best beloved human friend, when he suddenly saw Him in His glory, "fell at His feet as dead." Yes, but He is also all the while this "gentle Jesus, meek and mild."

And He likes to be with us all the days, and is never tired of it, all day long.

So it will be " to the consummation of the age." " The end of the world " is a phrase which gives us the conception of a final collapse of the universe. That was not in our Lord's mind in this passage. He referred to the end of *the æon*, between His first and second Comings. This æon, some of us think, is heading up now to its majestic close, when a new age will come in, of which the characteristic will be the manifestation of His presence after another mode, and a glorious one. But the point is this—that whatever be the needs of the present age, right up to its consummation, the Christ of God, not *will be*, but *is*, with us, every day and every hour, to be used as the loving, the willing, the delighting, " great Companion."

The last word shall be this. I ventured to speak on Monday night from the Obadiah text: " Possess their possessions." May I put beside that an appeal to my friends in Christ to give a further look in their Bibles over all the passages which contain, " *We have*," or kindred words ? " *We have* such a

High Priest"; "*We have* a High Priest who can be touched with the feeling of our infirmities"; "*We have* the Son, and having Him *we have* the life." It will remind us of our possession, and be a perpetual invitation to possess. And the possession, among other things, is this changeless Presence: "I am present every day, all the days, with their different colours, and all the hours, in all the things that fill them up." Having that great possession we will by His grace possess it, and He will be glorified in our use of Him. So be it, for our mercy, and to the fulfilment of His will of love, now and to the end.

www.ingramcontent.com/pod-product-compliance
Lightning Source LLC
LaVergne TN
LVHW021610080426
835510LV00019B/2503

* 9 7 8 1 4 9 8 2 9 2 4 9 8 *